LOVELY WITCHCRAFT

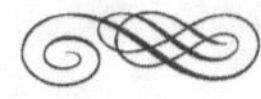

MEG

The Philomath's Ballad

LOVELY WITCHCRAFT

to eldest daughters.
to those in their "sad girl" era

Playlist

"Witchy Woman" by Eagles
"Ferris Bueller" by Emei
"Way Down We Go" by KALEO
"Bigger Person" by Lauren Spencer Smith
"Ophelia" by Lumineers
"the fruits" by Paris Paloma
"Irish Eyes" by Rose Betts
"Overwhelmed" by Royal & the Serpent
"Hazel Eyes" by Sabrina Jordan
"Quarter Life Crisis" by Taylor Bickett
"tolerate it" by Taylor Swift
"happiness" by Taylor Swift
"long story short" by Taylor Swift
"right where you left me (bonus tract)" by Taylor Swift
"cardigan" by Taylor Swift
"my tears ricochet" by Taylor Swift
"mirrorball" by Taylor Swift
"this is me trying" by Taylor Swift
"Anti-Hero" by Taylor Swift
"You're On Your Own, Kid" by Taylor Swift
"All Too Well (10 Minute Version) (Taylor's Version)" by Taylor Swift
"Never Grow Up (Taylor's Version)" by Taylor Swift
"Long Live (Taylor's Version)" by Taylor Swift
"Castles Crumbling (Taylor's Version) (From The Vault)" by Taylor Swift
"Young and Beautiful" by Lana Del Ray

Trigger Warning

These works of poetry speak a lot about being
the eldest daughter,
Anxiety, Depression, mentions self-harm,
and eating disorders.
More information can be found on the-philomaths-ballad.com
Please be safe while reading and enjoy.

Contents

I

coffee shop

i sat in the back,
coffee and laptop
on the table, earbuds
softly humming
some instrumental
music i had picked
earlier.

i guess it would work.

my foot shook as i thought
i felt eyes on me.

look up.
they're watching.
you look weird.
your hair is a mess.

your posture is bad.
they're judging.

i give in.
i look up.
only baristas left
in the cafe.
i was fine.
goddamn anxiety.

II

witchcraft

the candles were lit.
the salt circle was drawn.
the sage cleansed the air.
she sat, slowly waving the sage
and chanting.
her feet were bare and dirt clung
to soles from dancing in honor of
The Mother.

the candles slowly died out
as she sat, legs crossed, hands
sleepily resting on her knees,
her eyes closed as
The Mother
opened the universe to her child.

III

dear - -

i still remember you.
yes, i do.
i remember the trains
at christmas and how you went
inside for the fireworks.
i remember how lovingly
you took care of - -,
-, and -. i remember
your quietness and the respect
you gave others.

i went to dover air force,
you know? the museum is next door.
planes, history all over the property.
small rooms offered more stories.
you said very little about
your time in vietnam in the army.

i remember on veterans' day
when i would draw the badges
you would wear on a card for you.
i always saw it on the fridge.
it was always an honor to make the cards.

i touched the planes at dover.
each reminded me of you. each
reminded me of what you
sacrificed to keep this place safe.

i had always known you didn't want
to go. you had been drafted.
your number was in the paper,
losing the lottery no one wanted to play.

you went and joined the army.

i still remember you.
i still think about you sometimes.

thank you for your service.

IV

birch beer at Nana's

i sat in the living room
of the old blue house
behind Loyola, on the red couch,
barefoot,
the stale smell of
chocolate and cigarette
smoke filling my nose,
and Drew Carey asking contestants
to spin the wheel before the final showcase.

i stood, thirsty.

walking to the fridge,
opening the door,
looking for the golden
can with red lettering
amongst the red and white

cans of coke, the litters
of suburban almond smash,
the bottles of root beer,
and cream soda,
i found the last can
of birch beer.

V

dorian's portrait

he looked so small
as he curled into his hide,
cowering away from my outstretched
hands and cooing voice.
he laid cradled in my arms
like a newborn babe,
my knuckle rubbing his cheek.

he stood on his back legs,
looking at new world.

he sprinted around,
running in circles
before jumping out.

he slowly stopped cowering.

he slowly stopped running away.

he slowly started running towards
the door when i called him by name
or to give him pets.
he got impatient.
he begged for attention.

i could only smile and open the door,
watching him burrow,
watching his nose scrunch and twitch.
i could only giggle when he climbed on me,
his personal jungle gym.
i could only laugh when he jumped high
and twisted in the air, showing his glee.

he lives in a hutch at the base of my bed.
he lays and sits where he can watch me.
he runs up to say good morning to me.

his coat is soft.
his ears have turned grey,
as has his face,
only leaving most of him
a dusty orange brown.

he lays with me on the floor
after running until he can't.
he sits on my stomach and chest,
exploring the creature he is near.
he burrows,
planning another unsuccessful escape.

he runs up every morning to the door
when he hears me coo

good morning, Dorian.

VI

literature's lullaby

melancholy mistrials moaned
in sorrow as the star-crossed
lovers died in each other's arms.

sorrowful sparrows sang as Boo
crept back into his house,
disappearing again forever.

numb neighbors never watched
Daisy hit Myrtle with her car.

sullen Scrouge yelled
Bah Humbug
at his nephew.

malicious madness
struck Dorian as he destroys

the portrait he once loved.

aloof Alice got lost in Wonderland,
surrounded by cards.

golden gobs were below deck
as they sailed away
from Treasure Island.

the library fell quiet as the books
closed and the lights dimmed.
a glimmer of copper hair fluttered
out the doors, small pale hands
wrapped tightly around books.
she scurried down the stairs,
her candle drowsily dwindled.

VII

pomegranates

they were tiny red jewels, wrapped in white.
the juice dripped down her hand, flowing
in crimson streams as he placed a crown on her head.

she was a small, gentle blossom, contrasting
his dark, looming presence. he had offered
her something small to eat. the rebel child
ate six seeds, relishing in her freedom

during the cold seasons. she craved
his closeness and touch during the warmer
months when her mother tore them apart.

he missed his personal sunshine for the darkness
was suffocating. however, when the colder
months came, Demeter cried, Persephone
ran, and Hades met his dearest beloved at the gates.

VIII

portraits of music

symphonies of sapphire
crescendo across the canvas,
singing with scarlet,

mingling with magentas,
ignoring the indigo's ignorance,
frolicking with the forest green,

chasing the chartreuse,
running with red,
opening doors for ochre,

and laying with the lilac,
mingling on the canvas.

IX

their eyes

i drowned
happily
in the ocean
staring at
me.

i sunk
happily
into the depths
littered with
lights.

i drifted
happily
captivated by
the sweet
gaze.

X

philomath

sitting in a quiet corner,
surrounded by books,
in the back of the library,
nose deep in
Dickens,
Wilder,
Shakespeare,
Fitzgerald,
Faulkner,
Woolf,
Austen,
Bronte,
sits the philomath.

XI

monet

after *Water Lilies* painted by Claude Monet

the bridge sits amongst
the overgrowth of flowers
and mourning willows,
sheltering the small blades
of grass, protecting them.
the golden light sparkles
on the water as the cattails
worship the golden drops,
the fish dipping below the
lilies, lazily flicking their
tails as they follow the
gently soothing current.

XII

lazy sunday

the sun is too bright,
cascading through the
white sheer curtains.

the rooster is too loud,
cheering the sun to rise.

i can only cover my eyes
with the down pillows,
pulling the cotton sheets
over my shoulders, groaning
in protest.

the resilient sun ignored my
protests, touching things,
making them golden.

the joyous smell of coffee tried
to taunt me out of bed, your
voice trying to do the same.

good morning, my love.

XIII

redhair

it glows in the midafternoon sun,
ignoring the shades of chocolates,
chestnuts, ash, and golds, in long
copper strands. it taunts the ash
and chestnuts, allowing its glowing
crown to sit on top.

it's a beacon, catching the eyes of older men
and filthy questions.
its siren song isn't far off from earning
a whistle or a lustful gaze.
it's a heavy crown, one sometimes too
hard to carry.

it's a deceitful trophy,
one of great power and
turmoil.

XIV

snow

it came in droves,
covering the roads,
trees, cars, houses,
speeding up time
as it fell fast. the
wind whipped
the white powder
around, hiding
the fresh prints and
tracks of the wood
filled wheelbarrow.

XV

old library

the lights stay dimmed
as she slips through the
shelves, her skirt kissing
the edges of the archaic
leather, her blouse dusty
from the pile of books she
was shelving. her hair
tied up with a hair pin
through the middle of her
bun, a few pieces falling out
in front of her eyes. she blew
the pieces away, huffing when
they wouldn't budge. her heels
clicked across the tarnished
hardwood. her small, dainty
fingers gently parted the frail
hard covers, adding more to the

shelf before fixing her hair and
walking back to her desk, in
the middle of the library.

XVI

cold

it snakes up my spine,
constricting my body
into shivers. it swallows
me whole, not waiting
for me to fight back.

its venom sinks deep
below my pale skin,
bringing out the baby
blue tint of my veins.

it suffocates me,
ignoring my
struggles to get warm.

XVII

winter darkness

it crept up with no warning.
the blackhole swallowed me
whole, leaving me drowning
in my own thoughts. the sun
seemed...darker.
it didn't glow as bright.

each second dragging its feet,
not wanting to move as the clocks
yawned. nothing seemed bright.
every shade of blue was dark,
greedily sucking up light, keeping
it from the rest of the world.

XVIII

thinking

the idea was,
how should i put it,
perplexing.

how could my brain
put me into a spot
so black i couldn't see?

XIX

wildflowers

the field was wide,
stretching over
mountains, the soft
light breeze humming.
the sun ran its fingers
through the tall blades
of grass, settling down
calmly in the trees.
the petals sprinkled
through the air, riding
the breeze to the top of
the mountain, following
the curves Jord carved
last season.

XX

ballads

the sickly sad song
sighs as it slinks through
in sadness.

the people sit in large chairs,
staring at the floor, slightly slumped.

it slowly sinks in,
its sadness intoxicating.

XXI

clouds

i stare up at the sky
through the car's
sunroof, you on my left
in the driver's seat. i sat
as we talked, staring up
at the clouds, guessing
their shapes.

XXII

emerald eyes

you always complemented
my eyes. especially the shade.
you never failed to amaze me
with how you could describe
them.

you said they were
more priceless than
rubies and diamonds.
they were the most valuable
gem to you.

XXIII

incantaions

her hand shook as she lit the candle,
latin drippling over her chin.

the cat sat in the corner,
watching her as it curled into a ball,
eyes flickering to the girl in the circle.

the candle flickered as she pulled
her hands away,
waving the match in the air,
around herself and around the room.

the Mother was pleased,
showering her child with blessings,
offering guidance
as the white candle flickered
and the child made the flame dance.

XXIV

cacography

i stared in confusion
at my own notes,
scribbled in messy cursive,
just trying to get the words down.

the herbs and crystals sat
near the jar and burning incense,
begging for my attention.

the jars were cleansed
as was i and the room.

the Mother grew impatient
as she watched me try
to decipher my written notes.

XXV

solivagant

the walls closed in as i walked,
claustrophobia becoming my closest friend.

i was suffocating,
walking along the trails.

no matter when i reached out
i was met with silence.

so, as i tried to find the lit exit sign,
my legs carried on, tired, heavy,
ready to rest from wandering.

XXVI

deipnosophist

my father knows how to speak to people.
my father is the conversationalist.
like his father.
like his eldest daughter.

my father talks to everyone.

the cashier.
the teacher.
the dance teacher.
the bus driver.
the grocers.
the retail workers.
the bankers.
the other dancers.
the parents of the other dancers.
the store owners.

the child who thought he was santa.

just like his father and his eldest daughter.

XXVII

matutinal

my mother rises early.
she is commuting to work
with the sun. she opens
the office. she closes
the office. she makes
pancakes on sundays
and french toast on saturdays.
she fries eggs for my father,
popping the yolk more times
than not. she makes her coffee
before her children come downstairs
to a house smelling like cinnamon buns
on some saturdays. she has a banana
in hand as she kisses her children,
warmly asking them how they slept.

XXVIII

monopoly, the makebate

oh, sweet mother of death!

my father yells in protest as my sister laughs,
asking for rent.

take your blood money!

my mother sits at the other head
of the table, calling my father
by name as i roll the dice,
landing on my own property.
my father tries to trade
with free passes.

there are no free passes in monopoly.

XXIX

jackassery

hot rocks have been put into
my cousin's sleeping bags.
my cousin set his pants on fire.
my uncle has drunk milk past
the due date. my father has eaten
a cockroach on mistake.

all have been in the running
for the Darwinism award.

XXX

chevelure

my sister was born with hair.
i was born with whisps of orange
attached to my pale scalp.
my sister was born with
obsidian hair. i was born
with orange strands
that slowly grew to my
waist as i aged. my sister's
hair lightened to a deep
chestnut as mine darkened to copper.

XXXI

calefaction

she was curled in front of the fire,
her curly brown fur drying from
being out in the snow. she fell asleep
there on the rug after chewing on her
squeaky toy. she moved after we nudged
her to put more wood on the fire as she
lumbered outside before repeating the cycle,
staying near the fireplace.

XXXII

too much

i stood in the mirror,
staring at myself.
why couldn't i look
like the girls on those magazines?

i stood in the mirror,
staring at myself.
why wasn't i small
like the girls at school?

i stood in the mirror,
staring at myself.
was i too much?

i stood in the mirror,
staring at myself.
stomach too big,

shoulders too wide,
neck too short,
too many freckles,
breasts uneven,
nose too big,
lips too small,
eyebrows with no pigment,
forehead too large,
hands too small,
thighs too big,
s t r e t c h marks

everywhere.

XXXIII

aoibhneas

i stare out,
the birds flocking
in large black droves
around the graveyard.

they cover the backyard,
flying upwards as a unit,
never breaking.

the Morrigan watches,
sending the birds to watch
over her little warrior in training.

XXXIV

elysian

(adj.) beautiful or creative;
divinely inspired

you never fail to amaze me.

honeyed ice strands never lay right
when your hair gets too long. they
fall in your face and you look exasperated
whenever they fall in your eyes.

luminous light sapphire irises sparkle
back at me, full of agape and warmth.
they always soften after a small touch
or kiss.

your brilliance never dulls.
your brightness dazzles and delights.

my elysian love

XXXV

hurt feelings

i hadn't said a definite *yes* or *no.*
you assumed i needed to go to

urgent care

because i hurt a sixteen-year-old's feelings.

the fucking favorite
hurt again.
you take her side

again.

when have i ever told you no?
when was the last time i told you no?

when was the last time you celebrated with me?

when was the last time i didn't feel like a burden?
when was the last time i entered the house and felt at home?
when was the last time i came home and felt wanted?

apparently, my self-harm tendencies weren't
enough without the scars to prove it.
do you remember the night i told you?
you let it roll off your back like it was just
another day.
you couldn't even hide your disappointment.

did you ever ask my sister is she was anorexic?
no.
why would you?
she saw a dietitian,
cooked for the family,
made meal plans...
should i go on?
what did i do?
oh, never mind
because all you could see
was me in my bed,
curled up in a ball
while my stomach and back felt on fire
or when i didn't have the energy to move.
i'm clinically depressed or did you forget that?

while she exceled, you praised.
while i failed, you scolded.
you reminded me of my age.
you reminded me to act my age.
did you ever remember yours?

you agreed to get me a pet after my sister
had gotten two.

i was your first
but
did you want me?

XXXVI

my lady

my lady dressed in silk,
neck encircled with amber,
may your falcon cloak
carry you far.

my lady who offers me comfort,
housing the leaders of Ragnarök,
may the cats pull your chariot far.

XXXVII

the punching bag

can i have bad grades?
no.
can i go to a private school?
apparently not.
apparently, it gives me an attitude.
bad grades are out of the question.

you don't want to be a college dropout like me.
you have to take it seriously.
you don't know what hard is.
you have one job.

i bet the favorite never gets yelled at.
two years done and it should be celebrated.

midterms don't show what happened.
midterms don't show the hours cried.

midterms don't show the mornings
when I couldn't stand.
midterms don't show disappointment,
but you make yours known.

i asked you not to touch me, you did anyway.
i'm glad you have another child who you cannot make feel bad
about going to a private school.

yes, you know what i'm talking about.

three grand just for her schooling
every semester
because you wanted her to go to a Christian school.

we drive 20-year-old cars.

would it have made a difference if I didn't go to college?
i don't think it would have.

so I'll finish my degree
in four years
per your request,
hanging on by a fraying thread.

XXXVIII

parent's disappointment

did you ever stop to think
that i don't want to be stuck
in that bed all the time?

did you ever stop to think
that i want to be in the studio
and not missing practice?

did you ever stop to think
that i am terrified that i will
never get an answer for the pain?

do you complain about me to people?

do you complain about what i do around the house?

i take care of your mother-in-law

who you complain about.
if the kitchen isn't spotless, you complain.

your youngest child uses
every pot, pan, dish in existence
and if your eldest doesn't clean up
after her, you throw a fit.

i can sense how disappointed you are in me.
i can tell it runs deep.
i can tell i am not the child you wanted.

was i truly planned?
i can tell that you didn't want a broken child.

your youngest isn't mentally ill.
your youngest isn't physically ill.
your youngest doesn't have pain
that runs so deep that the soul cries.

did you try for another child
because you saw this happening?
did you try for another child
because i was too independent?

how often have you wished
you didn't have to take me
to blood work?
to get MRI's done?
to have EKG's?
to have x-rays done?
to doctor appointments?

to specialists?
to PT?

have you ever wondered
how much money you could've
saved without having to buy
all my medications?

i know how expensive they were.

she doesn't cause any extra issues.
no medical issues.
no mental health issues.
no physically issues.
no unwanted pain.
can manage money better than i can.

and looks like family when with you.

did you try for another child to get
a child that looks more like you two
instead of a milky, ginger, freckled child
who looks adopted?

your youngest looks like you two.

dark, almost black, brown hair,
can tan and missed the genetically
transmitted illnesses.

a normal child who doesn't have to worry
about her health.

doesn't look at a clock like it's counting down
to when she is using
a cane or
walker or
a wheelchair.
doesn't think time is passing
so fast that she wants to freeze it.
doesn't think about her body hating her
so much that it torments her, bringing pain.

did you keep me so i could be your disappointment?
did you keep me so the youngest
didn't know how that feels?
why did you want me in the first place?

why did you keep me?

XXXIX

second place

i'm first born
but second compared
to the young one.

second in everyone's hearts,
someone else always comes first.

only second place on the podium,
never good enough for first.

always second place,
never first.

will i ever be?

XL

depression & anxiety

i didn't ask for this.
she made her bed and
stayed there, dictating
when i would get out of mine.

there was no other way.
to not listen was stupid.
to not listen was pain.
to not listen was agony,
numbness.

she held the button
to my emotions with
an iron fist,
only to share it with her sister.

the controlling twins.

XLI

3 am

i stared at the ceiling.
awake for hours again.
does my mind have an
off switch?

i guess not.
gotta love insomnia.

sleep drains from my to-do list.
only thing I can do now is wait.
wait to fall asleep, wait to calm down.

the room is too warm, pillows aren't cold,
can't find a comfortable spot.

i walk to the window, open the shades
to search for the moon.

i couldn't find it amongst
the streetlamps crowding campus.

but i found a star,
said goodnight,
crawled back into bed,
fighting with the top sheet.

the only thing i can do is to hope
for is sleep before four.

XLII

dog on the bow

the mist covered the harbor,
lifting only enough to cover
the horizon. dinghies and motorboats
line the walkway below the gangplanks.

a small white dog bounced into his boat.
he pushed off, lowering the motor down
into the dark, clear water. the mutt's nails
clipped as he turned, standing on the far
most part of the bow before joining him
in the vessel. he roughhoused gently
before sailing off, lost from view,
obscured by the dock.

XLIII

the photographer

for a photographer on Captain John's Boats in Plymouth, MA

she sat on the old crates at the loading docks,
waiting to board. a paperback in hand, she pointed
at local relics for a woman from jersey. i sat,
listening, before jumping, diving into conversation
about books, buying, reading.

She recommended the bow, so we sat there.
her sunny energy was enough to lift the corners
of my mouth, curling them towards the sky.
a camera hung around her neck as she took
boarding pictures, a calm smile never leaving
her face.

may her nephews have the rich aunt she hopes to become.

XLIV

black cherry

for the receptionist at the Newport Lighthouse Cruise

round glasses perched on her nose,
her nails and hair both dipped
in black cherry red.

bright yellow, sunshine yarn
wrapped around knitting needles
in even rows as we discussed
swords,
baseball,
music,
books,
two english majors nerding.

XLV

blessing

the earth had cleansed itself,
Lady Gaia seeing the negativity.

the stiffness didn't affect me much
in the morning. the pain was lower
in the morning. my movement was better
in the morning.

i relished in the blessing.
the gods blessed today
with calm energy.

i shall relish in it.

XLVI

dumping ground

i was gone for a week.
it was obvious i wasn't
missed much. my room was
the dumping ground. the only thing
cleaned was the desk.

that held a
Bible,
laptop,
a sermon,
and some CS Lewis books.

none of which were mine.
laundry was all over my bed.
i couldn't walk into my own room.

yes, the large play area for Dorian was fantastic,

however, why the fuck did my room
become a dumping ground?
why couldn't you have helped to keep
it at least semi-organized?

i fold your laundry.
i put away your laundry.
hell, I'd never let one of your rooms
become that filthy.

i went into panic mode.
it stressed me out horribly.
vacation was quickly a thing
of the past as i hurriedly
organized my room so i
could have minimal peace
of mind so i could sleep.

XLVII

Icarus

he tumbled past Olympus,
and Apollo watched, wishing
he hadn't scorched the poor child.

Hebe shed a tear for the child as
he slipped past her grasp.
Eirene sent peace to Daedalus
as he watched his son fall from
the heavens.

Hermes paused, being told not to help.
Hades opened the gates of darkness,
Moros quietly setting his goblet down.

Dionysus paused, his goblet close to
his lips. Persephone waited for Charon
to arrive with Icarus.

XLVIII

eldest daughter chronicles

always others before yourself.
the therapist,
the nurse,
the care provider,
the protector,
the maid.

don't let your shoulders break
with the stress of responsibility.
don't step out of line.
be the example.
act your age.

teachers always say you have an old soul.
always well-behaved.
manners always in check.
nothing is to be out of place.

if anything isn't cleaned,
don't worry you'll be reminded
to do it until it's done.

can't leave home until everything
and everyone is taken care of.
can't leave without being worried
if something happens.

you wanted a son?
you had a son's name picked
from family names,
not out of a baby book.

i know how to
cook,
clean,
care for others,
care for children,
do laundry,
fix minor things,
change a lightbulb,
use a chainsaw,
use a backpack blower,
use many tools,
help fix things in cars,
how to hold a flashlight at the perfect angle
and move it for a better view,
build things from nothing,
disassemble things.

yet, my manners aren't up to par.
the kitchen isn't cleaned.
laundry isn't done.
the living room needs dusting.

i am awake prior to you.
i pass you asleep in your bed
until nine while i have been awake
and moving around since eight.

you haven't been home because work
doesn't let you have a break.

dishes have been run.
laundry is running.
i did clean the kitchen.
dishes were used.
they piled up near the sink.
laundry hasn't been done in a few days.
there is a lot of it.
the kitchen looks like tornado alley
because someone else cooked after i cleaned it.

i didn't mop the floors properly?
it's not up to your standards?
i tried my best.

i was the only one who cleaned.
i had to be the son you never had
and the daughter you got stuck with.

XLIX

attitude

whenever she has an attitude,
you never blink an eye.

when it's me,
hell freezes over.
when it's me,
it's a lecture.

what did we deserve to get this?
enough with the attitude.

you defend her.

mama bear **only** comes out for one kid.
mama bear always stays quiet
when the eldest needs support.

papa bear rarely comes out.
papa bear only comes out
when he's angry.

you ask why you deserve attitude.

i am the help, not your child.
i am second to everything,
even though i was born first.

L

money

it has never been lost on me
the concept of how expensive
it is to raise me.

the cost of
electric,
food,
insurance,
cars,
school,
phones,
laptop,
internet,
should i continue the list?

how about my medical bills?
my prescriptions?

i know it piles up.

you always remind me of the expenses of things.
you hold it over my head.

i know a new phone is five hundred dollars
with a trade in.
i know how much you liked not
having to pay for phones for a time.

i know how much my bill is for college.
please, don't remind me of your disappointment
when i don't do well.
there's more than one reason
why i don't want to be on medication.
were you hoping i would skip the autoimmune
gene so i wouldn't have to deal with it
or because it is expensive?

LI

suffocated

i was always called an "old soul".

anyone else the kid teachers wanted
in their class?
the one that was well-behaved?
quiet and answered questions well?
was polite and had impeccable manners?

the one no one knew was burnt out?
had no more motivation anymore?
didn't know what to do after school?

anyone else have an inner child screaming
to come out but has been pushed down so far
and shoved so far down that it can't be heard?

all because others come first.

all because you're the reason
the house isn't a mess.
all because you can handle yourself
and the other kid needs more.
all because you feel that you must
be protective of the other one.
all because the other one is now
your responsibility.

now you're twenty
and that "old soul" is fracturing quickly
while the inner child doesn't know how to grow.

LII

an ode to the eldest daughter

we are the in-house multi-tool.

the therapist,
the nurse,
the caregiver,
the protector of the young ones,
the planners,
the maid,
the one who makes sure everything runs smoothly,
the example,
the son our fathers wanted but never got.

we are the ones who get complimented
on our work ethic, our manners.
we hide our anxiety until it is the middle

of the night, and no one can hear us cry.
we pick up the slack, so it doesn't fall.
when we tell the truth it is not accepted.

but i see you.

i see the work you put in.
i see the fight you muster daily,
just trying to get through the week.
i see you trying to control chaos.
i see you trying to find who you are
and who you want to be.

you are not alone when you are crying
so hard with your hand over your mouth,
trying to keep quiet while your throat burns.
you are not alone when you feel guilty
for not doing things.
you are not alone when you feel as though
you come second to everything.

darling, you keep your head up
and your crown intact.

don't let anyone take it from you.

LIII

selkie's ballad

nectar dribbled from her vocal cords
and over her chin as she pulled herself
up to the small boat,

eyes piercing the royal and servant
rowing towards the shore.
the royal reached a hand to her.

her hair stuck to her;
the cold showed her no mercy.

the royal wrapped their cloak around her,
hiding her seal skin.

they held her close, nearing the shore.
her hair of gold flowed over her face,

the sun and freedom disappearing

as she entered the doors of the castle by the sea.

LIV

blackbirds

birds of ebony
cascade over the
blue skies of an early
october morning.

the rustling branches
woke me as you
were asleep beside me.

i tried not to wake you
as i walked to the window
to see the birds of ebony.

LV

deep creek

at the end of the road
sat a cabin.

a majestically crafted sanctuary,
filled with love.
grandkid art on the fridge,
a bear on the wall,
a turkey over the television.

let's not forget
the oil lamps on the mantel,
the framed photos on the table
behind the couch,
the hummingbirds always visiting
the hanging feeders,
classical music in the morning,
movies and shows at night after

a lovely dinner.

the time slowed,
the rooms were cozier,
the weather cooler.

just perfect.

the stone fireplace stood proud
in the living room,
a small, decorated wreath over
a large plain one.

the wooden mantel was somehow
attached, covered in small knickknacks
and fairy lights sat perfectly centered
between the vents just below almost identical rocks.

LVI

gnome garden

the little gnomes had moved upstream,
carrying toadstools only a few yards up.

they built a small town,
filled with a bakery,
a mill,
a blacksmith shop,
some tailors and seamstresses,
some cleaners, and a general store.

LVII

pelicans

the storm came hard and fast
before it blew over.
water still trickled from the sky
and wind chilled the air.

the pelicans didn't mind it.
they dove, circling for their next meal,
wings placed equal distance apart
from its body,
its long beak going into the water,
leaving only the tail above the surface.

LVIII

health care

you called it normal.
you said the heavy, painful periods
that i have always had were normal.
i thought different.
i told you i wanted to be tested.
you didn't listen.

when i was younger, i also had heavy periods.

were your cramps so bad you didn't want to move?
i leaked on the fucking regular and
you are telling me this is normal?

all i wanted was for you to listen
without looking like it is a chore to.
whenever i mention Hopkins,
you bring it back to how my medication will help,

you just might need a higher dose.
medication does not work for me.

it never has.

i made it clear that i didn't want the injections and why.
you didn't listen and brought it back to my medications.
why don't you hear me?

do you not hear me screaming out?
is my throat not raw enough?

LIX

contagious?

a little looked at me as i sat
on the floor of the studio.
yes, i had to explain why
i wasn't dancing.

pain is a bitch.

central pain syndrome never failed
to get in the way.

but, this way?
i will never forget.

are you contagious?

i almost cried on the spot.
but composure was everything,

only a laugh and a *no, i'm not*
could escape my lips.

i almost said something.
i didn't want to talk to the kid again.
i didn't want to make a scene.
i just left early.

the words followed me,
echoing until that was the only thing
i would hear while i cried in the shower.

LX

a fool's errand

it didn't exist.
i realize that now.
you made it seem real.
it seemed obtainable.

the right words,
the right gestures would unlock the key.

you made it seem like you enjoyed
my company, my friendship.
you were a comrade.

you sent me looking for more ways
to stay your friend.
more reasons to turn a blind eye
to you.

a laughable way to spend time,
running your fool's errand.

LXI

love or logic

we could make this work.
no, we can't. not in this economy.

well, how come? we know how to.
we would be so far in debt.

why do we have to wait?
you are trying to fill the void.

i have no void!
yes, you do.
it's dark, empty, cold.
it sucks every emotion out of you
and you cannot bring them back easily.

but look, i looked up how to make it work.
you aren't fucking listening.

we cannot do this. this will not work now.

but what if i will never be able to?

LXII

being twenty

am i supposed to be having fun while i'm twenty?
people party, drink, smoke.
go clubbing, are broke,
trying to find their way in the world.

am i supposed to have fun while i'm twenty?
i read, watch old movies,
will be in law school.

there is no time for
partying,
drinking,
smoking,
clubbing.

does the fun happen when i'm twenty-
one? or do i have to wait until i'm thirty?

LXIII

roomies

how many times have we watched
this show? who cares.
we are too busy looking at
photos of highland cows,
watching tiktoks,
getting work done,
reading,
talking.

but i wouldn't trade
the memories of
the hockey games,
the target runs,
the trips to noodles and co,
the dance parties,
all of us being up in the morning,
the loud sing-alongs,

the mini catapult.

you two have always made me laugh,
regardless of my mood,
always pushed me through the hard times,
and have become some of my best friends.

LXIV

late night gossip

do you remember when i beat you
at just dance?
okay, fine. it was once, but still.

do you remember all the photoshoots?
i still have those photos.

do you remember going to maine?
it was my first time on a flight.

do you remember going to the mall
and stopping only to window shop
or smell candles?

i remember when i first met you.
all the way back in middle school.

you still had your braces at the time.
i remember sitting and listening to you
practice piano.

you always play beautifully.
you have always stuck with me.
thank you, bestie, for all the memories.
here's to more.

LXV

fall semester

we had already planned
who was getting what.

we had picked the rooms.
we knew move in.

how could i contain my
excitement?

the end of august.
then i would be back.

end of august and i could
see them again.

four more weeks and gang would
be back together.

that's the thing they don't tell
you about when talking about college.

your roomies become some of your besties.

LXVI

h-

we went to the same high school.
i don't remember seeing you
in the hallways though.

i guess it was cause you were
a grade ahead of me.
no matter.

we had never met before
but i was excited to meet you.
you seem cool and our vibes

semi-similar.
you advised us on
picking the apartment.

you seem fun to be around

and i can't wait to
be your roommate.

LXVII

rings

i have had two identical
rings.

two claughdahs.

the original got eaten
by the drier.

the second sits on my right
hand.

a safety line,
a fidget,
a staple in my daily wardrobe.

it never leaves my finger unless
it must.

both purchased at similar places.
both reminders of how far i have come.

LXVIII

stanford prison experiment

i was assigned a number.
prisoner five.
i was no longer - -.
i was prisoner five.

the warden made sure
to remind me. the guards
reminded me.
if i messed up, i was a bad prisoner.

if i left, my other prisoners
were beaten.
if i left, well, i couldn't leave.
the shackles suffocated my ankles,

reminding me of what i had "done".
i missed home.

i wanted to go home.
i wanted home.

they threw me in the hole.
it was dark. only a sliver of light
came through the window

on the door. people tried to revolt.
they took turns beating us. this worked.
the warden was pleased.

LXIX

six months

in honor of d.b. and t.h.

half a year.

february was the last time.
the last time red beaded
over my scars and stretchmarks.

i shook.
i cried.
no one knew
i had done it.
i hid it well.

i cried when he saw them.

he was gentle,

running his thumb
over them.

she was patient while
i recalled the incident.
she felt it with me,
went through it with me,
validated the hurt.

occasional updates passed
during the weeks.

no incident since.

they helped me fight.
they helped me succeed.

this is for you, d.b. and t.h.

Acknowledgements

Thank you to family and friends for their support and encouragement while I write this. Thank you to all my creative writing teachers that I have had for helping me learn, create, and fine tune my skills. Thank you to the readers who have chosen my book to read. I wish you all the best.

The cover image is from the following website:

Social Media Pages

Instagram- @thephilomathsballad
TikTok- @redso14
Website- the-philomaths-ballad.com
Vocal- Megan Christopher

www.ingramcontent.com/pod-product-compliance
Lightning Source LLC
Chambersburg PA
CBHW052103150726
48002CB00006B/2191